Ephemera

Poems & Pictures

by Carina Pearson

WALNUT STREET
—PUBLISHING—

ISBN 979-8-9909790-2-4

Walnut Street
Publishing 1673
S Holtzclaw Ave
Chattanooga, TN 37404

Contents

Thank you to Walnut Street Publishing for believing in local artists and championing their art, and thank you to Wanderlinger Poetry Circle for these poems, for existing, and for giving me one of the best years of my life. I love you. You are magic.

Anew

Look to the horizon line.
The sky presses against the sea
in a perpetual kiss.

The weeping woman came running
with her face in her hands
towards the waves.

Who hasn't longed to begin anew?

Body whole,
heart unaching?

Heels in the sand,
soles to the surf,
while waves wash you clean:

anew
anew
anew...

Look to the horizon line.
The sea receives the sky
in a perpetual kiss.

River

Inside me is a river. As is in you.

Who are you, or I, to decide how it flows?

Perhaps you watch it,

the crashing white,

the ferocity,

the force,

brown leaves grieving for the green they once were,

the occasional dead fish,

the spider who hung too close whisked away.

You are you to say it shouldn't be so? Who am I to say it shouldn't
be?

It has its purpose, brutal or not.

Ellipsis

The cold paints everything technicolor.

Cotton candy blooms nod
while wind whispers to trees;
bright violent blue clashes with rust red and
I absorb hungrily.

What is life if not this?

Quiet wonder
private enduring
moments of rapture

The insistent on and on -
the pages of days –

en route to the final mark:

Comma, semi colon, period, ellipsis.

Which one will finish us?
I hope for an ellipsis...

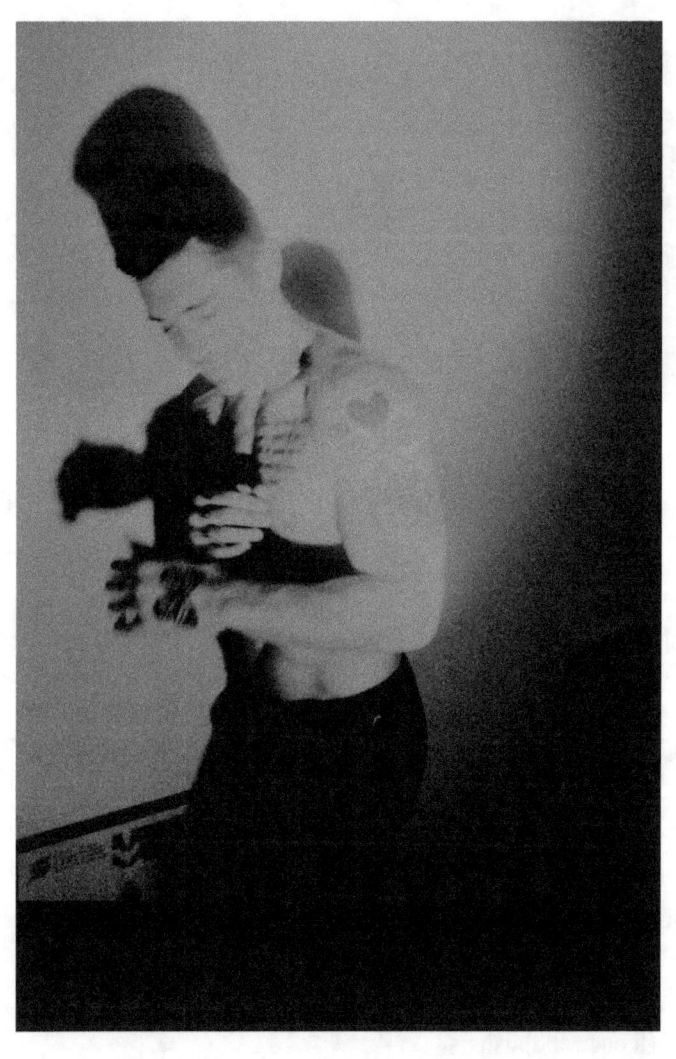

West Virginia

I remember the warm light. I was nine. I was chewing big red gum. The road was loud and ivory dust clouded the wheels. I had been in the way back with my map and my bear and his/her little clothes. You ran up to me and hugged me and we jumped together while we hugged. We talked about swimming in the river. The light glittered through the tall trees. I remember feeling like the sky knew me. I remember feeling big and important, before I got older and that notion was taken. I've since learned that you can be big and important, but only in the eyes of a few people, and only if you're lucky enough to find them.

Homesickness

Living is a slow accumulation.
A bone that aches,
the incision healing,
conversations that can't be un-had,
homes that no longer feel like home,
screws and plates inserted.

Various google searches:
how to forgive yourself for stupid mistakes,
DIY mosaics,
names of people you once knew,
recipes for shortbread.

I miss home and I
hadn't realized I even had one
until now.

Light Girl

The desire to please.

Did it start as I stood on the ladder at 6 years old
to reach the light string
in my father's dark room?

Dad would say

"Ok light girl,"

and I would pull the string with a click.

The bath of chloride and bromine
brought eyes and lips and faces into view
like ghosts appearing.

And dad would pull his photographs from the pools and clip them to lines.

The sudden spill on the floor was my fault.
I'm sure he was kind and calm about it all.

But that's what I remember most —the puddle on the floor.

18

Wick

Your heart - the tender little flame

trembling at the end of the candle-

warm, gentle, quiet-

could destroy us both,

could blacken beams,

tumbling them over below.

A flash-over could take our ceiling

should you choose.

So you keep to your wick

and I to mine,

and so our house remains upright,

and so our light continues,

a dim and lovely yellow.

The Promise of a Closed Box

Nothing haunts like why.
Why?
My fingers hurt from digging bare handed.
Tiny rocks redden the tips.

I scrape and scrape...
someone
told me that why
was buried in this yard.
They told me and I believed them.
What other choice did I have?

God talks to other people
but he won't talk to me.
I don't know why.
The wanting to know is so deep
that I can barely admit it's even there.
Why know why?

I don't need to know,
devil may care...
hand me another drink,
give me another kiss,
pay me another dollar.

I'll be fine.

Nothing.
Haunts like why.
The most horrifying why,
lying, I figure, at the center of the earth-
the why of our being-
being here,
being at all...
the why of the why of the why of the why

I hear there's a book
thick with tissue paper layers,
glints of gold on their edges,
covered in delicate black words
neat as a pin.

I could look for why there.
I've been advised to,
but the terror that I won't find it there
keeps me from reading it,

Like a box unopened
as I desperately want it to contain jewels.
If it remains closed,
There's always the chance that it does.

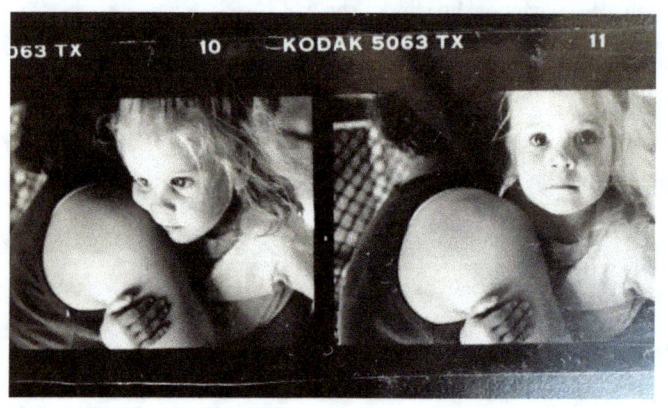

Dream No. 1

In this dream you come to me and say, "There's a train coming and we're gonna go watch it." I say ok and follow. We sit on the side of the tracks. The air smells like crushed brown leaves and a fire somewhere in the distance, which always has the effect of making me grateful I exist. We watch the train pass and the steel whines under the weight of the cars. You ask me are you always this sad and I say yes sometimes not really. You tell me to let myself be sad and quit making it worse by fighting it. I say ok. After that we sit for the longest time in silence, but the warm kind that envelops like a shower curtain. You need to take direction from someone else instead of always yourself you say. I say ok. The dream ends.

Pulse, as in
yearning, Ache, as in longing,
dreaming as in envision, mist, as
in containment, memory, as in
bliss, indigo, as in bathing,
balm, as in your
gaze ...

Dream No. 2

In this one the sky is glowing cobalt. I go out onto the deck and I can feel that you're following. I'm wearing a dress made of black silk. There's a sense of the immediate. There's a warm wind strong enough to push against with all our weight. I lean over the railing to feel the thrill of almost falling. The horizon is a clean sharp blade cutting the blue. I imagine what the blade is saying and my brain responds, "chase forever in the everlasting repeating here and now here and now here and now here and now." You turn to me and say, "I'll count. You hide." You close your eyes and start counting. I take off my heels and run inside and down the stairs. My heart beats loud and fast. I find a closet and curl myself up in it.

I Want to Ask You

I could ask "how are you?" but

I'd rather ask:

Do you ever find yourself stunned to be in a body with limbs and
fingers you didn't fashion...

with feelings so huge

and longings so red

with a want to hold and be held in a way that is holy and
undeniable...

without any idea of where it could possibly all come from?

Do you ever feel the mundane is a slow drip of poison and want
relief?

Do you ever get the urge to jump off a small cliff and feel the cloud of
bubbles fizzing against your skin,
or drop head first off a diving board,
scary fun and confusing,
not knowing which way is up?

Tell me, do you ever want to drive for hours and hours to a field
somewhere

and feel yourself small against the vast expanse, remote and alive...

Do you ever want to wipe the board clean of every pain and ache and rejection and disappointment you've ever had?

Nothing left but pure white gloss,

every possibility open again,

like a window...

Do you ever?

Cathedral

I need to be much smaller.

I wish I could know you

as microbes rushing in your blood know you -

wandering chambers

in that grand cathedral of bone

you carry atop your neck.

Maybe it would feel like completion,

or an arrival,

a merging...

My aloneness -

burden/haven -

oscillating back and forth,

a pendulum

hypnotizing.

Please go away and view me from a safe distance.

Unless, that is,

I can enter your ear and peek inside to verify

that we are not so different,

and I am not so alone,

and neither are you.

I'm a professional I promise

I'm a professional I promise.
Look at this stupid little plastic card I have dangling
in this clear envelope thing
that has my picture on it and my name that proves
I'm a real person
and I have a right to be here because I've done all
the steps and I have the papers and I filled out the
forms - so many forms -
and I show up every day at the right time and I
comb my hair
and I know some stuff some important people in
white rooms told me
and I try to apply it and I'm definitely never full of
fear and confusion and
I definitely never feel like *what am I doing* and
I definitely never feel like this is all just an
elaborate play that some people made up and
it's not like I hate the play or even that I think
there's not a point to the play
but it's still just a play
and we could've made up a different kind of play -
is it a drama, is it a comedy? -
it changes every hour and
I'm just trying to figure out my role in it, like my
placement on the stage, or the blocking , or the next
line,
but regardless I do have this badge and on the days
when I feel like a child I wear it, like today, because
I'm a professional I promise.

34

Birds

I'm exhausted of myself, are you?
Let's try being birds.
Let's sit in the triangular awnings beneath the walking bridge and
watch brown water flow below.

No self-image,
memories,
or guilt.

Only silence, pure and thick as cream.

I could be embarrassed of the need for myth, but it's woven into me,
into you, into us.

As birds though, the only meanings:

River turns to gold glitter at sunrise.
Gentle wind today.
Glistening pink worm.
Found napkins for nest.

I'm exhausted of myself -
there's no escaping her...
she and I in this small closet of bone
peering out at the world
wondering
what is all this?
And the questions never ever end...

I'm Waving Hello

This very second -
more intimate with you
than clothing
than skin
than breath…

small enough to sit on
the head of a pin,

will not hold still.

Move to catch it and find
it flutters in your hands
flying from them
away into memory,
distant.

Through the picture window of your mind's eye, I'm waving hello,

as if to say

I miss you, I miss this - these walls and floors, this specific sort of
somethingness -

us as we were now.

This very second will not hold still,
a small animal
frightened,

She barrels on like rapids -
beautiful and relentless.

This very second,
sense it now.
She is precious if for no other reason
than one day we'll look around and find
that all of this has changed.

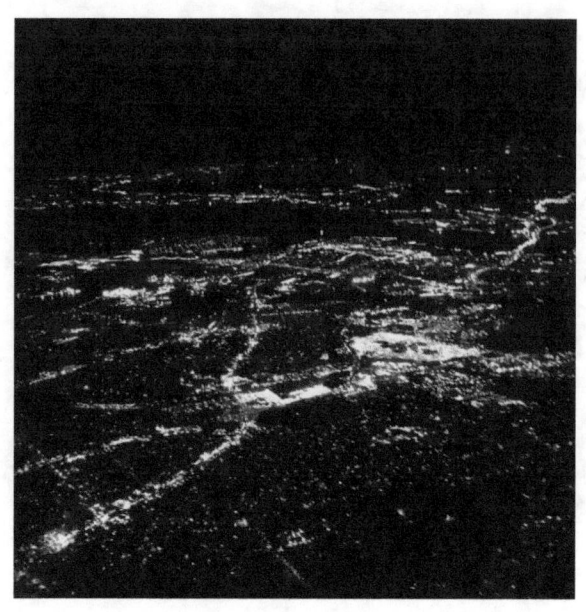

In a Plane Overlooking a City at Night

I never feel more small and

in awe than when I'm overlooking all those tiny lights...

the doll houses each enclosing people not unlike me,

with longings and fears and faces

I'll never know.

How bewildering and vast the ocean of humanness.

It goes and goes and goes...

Once, in Memphis

What is blood if not silken,
if not scarlet,
if not warmth,
if not essence?

I was jealous, that day in Memphis, when my friend Natalie shared
that

once,
a lover has traced her veins with his finger
saying,

"See? This is your life."

Romance is being deeply perceived.

Some Wonder

After rejections and harms unseen,

after enduring the mundane and the awful,
you lug your tired body from bed

like a wounded soldier

to do the day.

Illnesses have arrived with their

various indignities and flavors of suffering.

And yet...

look at you here–

eyes open,

unfolding,

bearing witness,

hoping,

enduring.

Some wonder, you are.

Drinks with Sarah

At night we meet in dim rooms
to drink purple drinks with flowers floating in them -
feminine potions for bloodletting.

Whiskey or gin pulls
some unseemly desire or jealousy
from my mouth

and you just say

"Of course."

That phrase,
a gentle hand pressed against my heart.

"Of course,"
Both wolves are present -
so which one to feed?

"Of course,"
that ugly thought,
that fear of being overwhelming and underwhelming,
of being bad...

"Of course" -

As if to say:

your being human is as inevitable as

a river's running.

So easy to tell others "of course," and
so difficult to tell myself.

But maybe I have you for that.

Pinball Machine

Inside me is a violence of desire.

The bar is ever rising -
never enough.

Pretty enough, smart enough, kind
enough, fulfilled enough, driven enough...

Why are we like this?
I'm sorry friend.
I wish rest for us.

Lately I look into the window above the sink and see a face I've often
seen -
sometimes looking older,
sometimes like a child,
but why should I care what she looks like day to day?

I was made to experience;
I wasn't made to be an object, or a factory.

I was made to wander between random buildings
on a gray day
and think things like:
What's behind that door?
Or maybe I'll try their coffee.
Or maybe I'll sit here and gaze at this tree with its plum colored
leaves...
and oh to bathe in that color,

or wear it as perfume,
or drink it like syrup…

I was made to thrill at whiffs of gardenia
that kiss me unexpectedly in parking lots,
or wonder at the brutal beauty of gasoline,
all glistening oil
the color of beetles' wings.

To be in random places at random times among random strangers
because honestly -
what is this huge chaos pinball machine and
how did we all end up inside it?